Write Your Life Story in **28** Days

Dee Dees

authorHOUSE®

AuthorHouse™
1663 Liberty Drive, Suite 200
Bloomington, IN 47403
www.authorhouse.com
Phone: 1-800-839-8640

© 2008 Dee Dees. All rights reserved.

No part of this book may be reproduced, stored in a retrieval system, or transmitted by any means without the written permission of the author.

First published by AuthorHouse   4/28/2008

ISBN: 978-1-4343-7715-9 (sc)

Library of Congress Control Number: 2008903036

Printed in the United States of America
Bloomington, Indiana

This book is printed on acid-free paper.

Table of Contents

Introduction vii

Chapter 1   In the Beginning 1

Chapter 2   The Joy of Research 5

Chapter 3   Get Organized 9

Chapter 4   Writing 13

Chapter 5   Day by Day Exercises 23

Chapter 6   Week One 25

    Day 1 – The Vital Statistics and Life List
    Day 2 – Make a Time Line
    Day 3 – Places You've Lived / Schools Attended
    Day 4 – Jobs Held
    Day 5 – Achievements/Accomplishments/What You're Proud Of
    Day 6 – About Your Parents
    Day 7 – About Your Grandparents

Chapter 7   Week Two 41

    Day 8 – Childhood/school days
    Day 9 – Childhood: Birth to 12 (outside of school)
    Day 10 – Special People
    Day 11 – Grade School

Day 12 – Teen Years
Day 13 – High School (Grades 7 - 12)
Day 14 – College/Advanced schools

Chapter 8   Week Three 59

Day 15 – Career and Family
Day 16 – First job / Military
Day 17 – How you met your spouse - Courtship - Wedding
Day 18 – Early Family Life - Before Children
Day 19 – Children
Day 20 – Special Occasions
Day 21 – Proudest Achievements

Chapter 9   Week Four 75

Day 22 – Travels: Highlights of places you've visited
Day 23 – Clubs/Organizations/Civic involvement/Volunteerism
Day 24 – Retirement and Grandchildren
Day 25 – Reflections
Day 26 – The World Around You
Day 27 – Catch-up Day / Where Are They Now?
Day 28 – Letter(s) to Loved Ones

Chapter 10   Fun stuff 91

Chapter 11   Finishing Touches 95

Chapter 12   The Next Step 99

Appendix 101

Your Timeline
Mind Mapping Example
A sampling of descriptive words

Introduction

"Words are the only things that last forever."
William Hazlitt

Why write your story?

For over 10 years, I've been teaching people, through classes, workshops, and my book "LifeNotes," how to write the stories of their lives. Before beginning, they often see the project as an overwhelming process, which will take years to complete. I usually manage to convince them that it doesn't have to be that daunting.

Taken in small steps, with a plan and incremental goals, anyone – and yes, I mean *you* – can create a fairly comprehensive overview of a lifetime in just a few weeks.

We all have a treasure chest of experiences – or stories – that have made us *who* and *what* we are. Unfortunately, most of those stories go untold, and our descendants are left with their assumptions, guesses, and limited – often inaccurate – information about us.

But many of our experiences can provide insightful lessons for those who follow. Others may just provide entertainment or enlightenment. In any case, recording our memories provides a continuity between our past and our future, our ancestors and our descendants.

Why this book?

I once sent my Grandmother a list of questions about her life, for her to answer whenever she felt the urge. I wasn't sure if she would ever actually do anything with it. But to my delight, when I visited her on her ninetieth birthday, I found the questions there on her kitchen table, almost half of them answered. For the next several years, she continued writing bits and pieces of her life's stories, providing me with an insight into her life I'd never had before. It was like finding a buried treasure! *(On May 1, 2007, she turned 101, and was still telling me stories whenever I'd visit!)*

Her stories provided me not only with entertaining reading but a better understanding of her life as a child, and, to some extent, why she had become the person she was. As I asked her for more details about some of the topics, she provided even more background. I was overjoyed to learn so much of her past, and in a sense, my own past.

Years before, soon after my children were born, I had considered writing about some of my experiences. But it seemed so overwhelming that I kept putting it off. Finally, once I had a computer, I decided there was no longer any excuse for not writing about my life, so I began; "I was born in Washington D.C. in 1944."

Next came information about my parents, where we lived, the school I attended, and who my friends were. It didn't take me long to see that this was really boring. Why? It was not a collection of my stories at all, but only a recitation of facts, names, places and dates.

While these facts and data are important to include, I quickly realized that it was the stories, more than the data, that made me who I am. So I began making a list of experiences I wanted to write about, such as playing near a creek as a child, how I felt when a special aunt died of cancer, and the four years I spent working in Viet Nam. As I made brief notes about the experiences, I realized how much fun it was going to be to share my *stories* with my children and future grandchildren.

My goal with this book is to make it as user-friendly and how-to oriented as possible, with little of the theory and philosophy that tends to get us bogged down. Before beginning my writing journey, I once spent a week reading a detailed book about how to write a family history. When I was done, I was so overwhelmed that I never actually started writing. That's why this is intended to help you begin *right now* to capture memories of your experiences and stories and to get them down on paper.

This book will help you take what may seem like an overwhelming task – writing your *life* story – and divide it into small, manageable chunks, writing *one story at a time*.

If you follow the schedule and guidelines, in four weeks you can have a comprehensive overview of your entire life. But don't feel you need to stop there! As you write, you will probably continue to remember other events, other people, other situations, you will want to include. The hundreds of included topic questions will help you with this.

My hope is that you will continue adding to your life story as long as you continue your life. Your children, grandchildren, and many generations to come, will all thank you!

Chapter 1

In the Beginning

"If you would not be forgotten, as soon as you are dead and rotten, either write things worth reading, or do things worth the writing."

Benjamin Franklin

You are about to embark on an exciting journey – into your past! I'm sure you'll have many wonderful memories; some will be of experiences and people you may not have thought about in years. Write about the good times, the bad times, the everyday times. Write about things you may not have been able to talk about before, for whatever reason. Write about experiences that others may learn from. Write to provide a history of your family. But write! It will be a wonderful journey for you, and a treasured work of love to hand down to your descendants.

And remember, the exercise of writing one's experiences is not just for those in their "golden years," it's for everyone! What better time for a young Mom or Dad to begin writing about their life together, than when they're just beginning their family, and the memories of those wonderful experiences are fresh in their minds? The few minutes spent recording precious memories as they happen, will soon add up – and the result will be a complete personal and family history in years to come.

Whoever you are, wherever you are in life, begin now to record the stories of a lifetime – *your* lifetime!

SET A GOAL

This book is a goal in itself. Write Your Life Story in 28 Days. It's a challenge, and a promise, but only if you do the work. Set a goal right now to schedule an hour or so each day to get the job done. You wouldn't have bought the book if you didn't think you could do it. So right now, make an appointment with yourself. Whether it's at 6:00am, or 10:00pm, or sometime in between, write it on your calendar, and *do it*. Everyday! No procrastinating! Just do it!

BE ACCOUNTABLE TO SOMEONE ELSE

Some people need a little nudge to make them accountable. Tell your spouse, partner, or someone else close to you to make sure you follow through with this project every day. Or gather a few people together to meet once or twice a week. At that time you can discuss your progress, what challenges you might have and how others have handled those challenges. Perhaps you'll even want to read some of your stories to each other for feedback.

WHY 28 DAYS?

Having a set time frame often helps us achieve a goal we might continue to procrastinate doing if there were no deadline – even if it's a self-imposed deadline.

I once wrote a novel in 30 days, because it was an online project. The object was to write a 50,000 word novel during the month of November (www.nanowrimo.org) Though I came short, only writing a little over 48,000 words, I still had written the story I'd been thinking about for a couple of years.

Did I fail because I didn't reach the 50,000? Not at all. I did indeed have the basis for a novel, with a beginning, middle and end, and a pretty darn good story line. At some point (when I set another deadline for myself!) I'll go back and flesh it out, edit and polish it, and publish it. The point is the narrow time frame and the challenge of meeting it is what got the story written, and I dedicated several hours each day to writing an average of 1750 words per day.

Another reason for the 28 day time frame is that anyone can do just about anything for only 28 days. It doesn't seem as overwhelming as devoting a year or two of our lives to a project.

Lastly, studies have shown that if you do something consistently for 28 days, (some say only 21 days) it will become habit. So even after you've "finished" the book of your life's stories, you may feel inclined to continue writing one or two stories a day about the topics you didn't have time for within the initial goal period. In other words, keep on writing!

HOW THIS BOOK WILL WORK

Week 1 - Data

During the first five days, you will mostly be compiling data to help you with the rest of the assignments. Some will only take 15 minutes or so, some a bit longer. None should take more than 1 hour.

On the sixth and seventh day you will begin actually writing descriptions. The writing time itself will probably not take more than an hour a day, but you may spend more time than that thinking about what you want to say. Don't agonize too much over getting it just right – you can always go back after the 28 days and edit or change whatever you want to.

Weeks 2, 3 and 4:

These chapters will consist of more writing, with a couple of exceptions to make lists, when necessary.

Each daily assignment will include the following:

- A daily goal for you to achieve
- Some tips for writing on the assignment
- One or two suggested assignments, in case you aren't sure what to write about. These will usually be events or times that your descendants will most want to know about. (i.e. meeting your spouse, choosing your vocation, achievements of which you're most proud.)

In addition, some chapters will include Topic questions. If you're not sure how much to include in a suggested topic, the questions will help you get a lot of the details down. Don't feel you have to answer all of them; in fact many of them may not even apply to the topic you've chosen to write about. They're just there as another aid in case you get bogged down. Even when writing on a topic from your own memory, look at the suggested questions to see if there's more you can add.

Scattered throughout the book are several pages for you to record your own memories or make notes. The suggestions given are generic; yours will be specific to your life.

For instance, a topic from the list might be "Tell some experiences from grade school," and you might write on your list "The bully who stole my lunch later taught me how to stand up for myself."

Chapter 2

The Joy of Research

> *"If you're not having fun, you're not doing it right."*
> Helen Blanchard

When you're writing your stories, there may be lapses in your memory as to exactly what happened, who was there, or where it took place. To fill in the gaps, get involved in doing some research. Talk with others, track down records, go to reunions, and get in touch with family members you haven't seen for a while. Get the impressions of others. Borrow letters, pictures and scrapbooks from other family members to help jog your memory. You might even want to research the origin of your family name.

For major events, look up old news articles at the library. Research librarians can be a great help by telling you where to find any public information you may need. And, of course, if you're familiar with the internet, you'll find a wealth of information on-line.

If you feel you'll want to do research, you may be tempted to start before beginning the 28 day writing period, so you don't get bogged down. But if several weeks go by and you haven't yet begun the research, then just make the decision to start writing. You can always go back and do the research later. The important thing is to begin *now*, getting your stories down for future generations.

WHERE TO LOOK FOR MEMORIES

WHAT YOU MIGHT HAVE ON HAND

Go through your house looking in the basement, attic, closets, files, trunks and storage boxes. Gather as much as you can that you feel might help in your search for facts, or just to jog your memory. If you can, put everything that might be helpful in one place, whether a box, a file cabinet or a closet. Here's what to look for:

- √ Birth & Marriage Certificates
- √ Passports
- √ Diplomas
- √ Certificates / Awards
- √ Deeds
- √ Estate Records
- √ Letters from others
- √ Diaries and Journals
- √ Budget & tax records
- √ Canceled checks
- √ Funeral programs
- √ Wedding invitations
- √ Family papers
- √ Mementos from trips (hotel receipts, sightseeing brochures)
- √ Photographs
- √ Scrapbooks
- √ School yearbooks
- √ Tape recordings (audio & video)
- √ Home movies
- √ Miscellaneous mementos and souvenirs

WHAT YOU MIGHT HAVE TO HUNT FOR

This will be a little tougher, but may only be necessary if you want to dig way back into your family history and genealogy. If you're only telling stories from your personal experience, you won't need to do this. But if you need to verify dates, names or places, here are some places to try. Much of this can be found on the internet, either through public records, or by joining one of the several genealogy web sites, such as Ancestry.com or FamilyTreeMaker.com.

- √ Birth, Death & Marriage records
- √ Cemetery records
- √ Immigration & citizenship records
- √ Historical Society records
- √ Newspaper archives
- √ Pension & job applications
- √ Judicial records
- √ School records
- √ Military records
- √ Church records
- √ Census records

WHAT OTHERS MAY HAVE

Contact friends, relatives, former coworkers, doctors, neighbors, etc. Ask for letters you wrote to them, copies of documents, pictures, or whatever else might help you. Develop a questionnaire that applies to what you want to know. Ask for their memories of you as a child, the type of person you were, as well as stories they remember about you that you may have forgotten. Some items you might gather from others are:

- √ Letters and cards from you
- √ Home movies and/or audio tapes
- √ Photographs
- √ Documents
- √ Their memories!

Chapter 3

Get Organized

ORGANIZING YOUR MATERIALS

Before starting, you'll want to gather a few simple materials so you can stay organized.

- Three-ring binder
- 12-18 Tabbed dividers with pockets
- Notebook paper

You may also need a three-hole punch if you're writing on a computer, so you can punch the pages as you print them out and add them to the binder.

On the tabbed dividers, you will want to label them with some of the following categories. You can do this before starting, or as you go. Typical categories might be: Early Childhood, School Days, Military life, Family Life, etc.

The daily exercise topics will give you some ideas about how to divide your stories, so that when you're finished with all the writing, you'll be able to put them in an order that makes sense to you.

Feel free to come up with your own sections, too. For instance, someone who spent several years working in Europe, might have a section labeled "My years in Europe." This is *your* book - make it work for you.

STORING YOUR MATERIALS

Depending on how much "stuff" you accumulate, there are several ways you can store and organize it. Beginning with the simplest...

- √ Pocket dividers in a three-ring binder. (This would be a separate binder from the one you'll put your finished stories in.)

These types of dividers, as well as clear page protectors, can be purchased at office supply and most large variety stores. Label the tabs in any way that will help you find items easily. Some categories might be:
- Awards
- Newspaper clippings
- Letters
- Documents
- Photographs

- √ Accordion file

These are readily available in variety or office supply stores. They expand to hold quite a lot, and have built-in tabbed dividers for sorting your materials.

- √ Storage box with file folders

You might choose either a plastic box with a hinged lid, or a cardboard storage box with a lift-off lid. Either one will hold hanging folders, and will hold much more than the two methods above.

ORGANIZATION CATEGORIES

- √ Type of materials: i.e., Genealogy, legal, personal notes, correspondence, etc.
- √ Periods of life: Childhood, teens, adulthood, parenthood, retirement
- √ People: yourself, spouse, parents, children, friends, acquaintances
- √ Locales: Hometown, current residence, travels, etc.
- √ Events: School days, family celebrations, accomplishments, careers
- √ Jobs

You might think of other ways to organize and store all the notes, pictures and documents that you collect. Do whatever works best for you.

NOTE: *Please don't let the above lists overwhelm you or deter you from beginning to write. You might do perfectly fine writing from your memories alone, without any backup materials. Just begin writing, and if you find you need more information on a particular topic, you can begin looking then.*

Chapter 4

Writing

ORGANIZING YOUR THOUGHTS

Okay, so you're probably thinking; *"I don't know where to start or what to write about."* It's the standard "writer's block" that many of us struggle with when taking pen to paper.

Or you may be thinking *"I haven't done anything interesting; My life was boring; Who will care about my life."*

Stop that kind of thinking right now! Once you begin writing, you will realize your life was way more interesting than you thought. You have faced challenges, overcome struggles, enjoyed successes, and had some good times in your life. Even some of the bad times will have made you stronger, and taught you lessons.

Don't worry about not being able to think of what to write about. Each section will provide lots of topic questions to stir your memory. Most topics will apply to just about everyone, but there will also probably be many questions that won't apply to you.

Since every individual's life is unique, you will have had lots of experiences that won't be covered by any of these questions. One of the exercises for Day 1 will give you an opportunity to begin a list of your specific memories. So, even before looking at the topic questions in the following chapters, you'll have a list of your unique experiences and memories.

Photo Albums

Another option is to flip through some of your photo albums for topics to write about. You'll be surprised at the number of additional topics you will come up with. After all, if the event was important or interesting enough to photograph and save, it's probably worth a story!

Time Line

A Time Line can be helpful in recording important events in your life, as well as documenting historical events that happened during your lifetime. You will create your own on Day 2.

Looking at each year might remind you that you took your trip to Italy just before Kennedy was shot, or that 1958 was the year you broke your arm learning to ski.

Even if you don't come up with any new topics for stories, it's fun to see an overview of the highlights of your life this way.

The Craft of Writing

Once you have a list of your personal topics, or if you're using a topic from the following chapters, you'll want to write a story around it. This sometimes seems like the most difficult part of getting started. Here are some tips to help.

Expanding Your Answers

Sometimes we know the short answer to a topic, but we can't quite think how to expand it to add more detail.

The questions in the following chapters will help you with that. Initially, when reading a question, you might jot down a short answer to it. But... *AND THIS IS IMPORTANT...* DO NOT just leave it at that. Rather, look over your answers and see how you can weave them into a cohesive story. For example, the following seven questions are in the section "On My Own." An example is shown as to how you might jot down a note about the answer.

The next section shows how to develop a story from these answers.

How did you meet your spouse?	*At a party*
What was your first impression?	*I didn't like him.*
What was your courtship like?	*We mostly went to movies and skating*
When did you know this was "the one?"	*After about 3 months*
How long did you date before becoming engaged.	*4 months*
Describe your proposal; where, when and your memories of it.	*He proposed on September 16th, 1959, at a restaurant in Atlanta.*
How long was your engagement?	*8 months*

Now, this provides information, but it's kind of boring to read. To make it more interesting, take the same information and weave it into a narrative.

The example below shows how the answers become a story. The underlined sections are from the actual answers to questions above.

If you feel, as many people do, *"I'm not a writer, I don't know how to start,"* just begin as if you're writing a letter to a friend you haven't seen in years, telling about the important events in your life.

> *I met Jim in <u>May of 1959</u> at a <u>graduation party</u> given by mutual friends from college. At first I thought he was silly and childish because he was trying to be funny all the time. <u>I didn't care for him at all in the beginning.</u> When he invited me out for hamburgers, I almost said "No," but I wasn't dating anyone else, and thought at least it would get me out of the house, and a free meal is a free meal. And he was funny - if in a silly way. After the first date, I slowly came to like him more, and realized his silliness was a way of getting attention, and once he knew I liked him, he didn't have to try so hard. We <u>saw movies, went roller-skating and boating</u>, and occasionally went out to dinner. It only took about <u>three months of dating</u> before I knew he*

Dee Dees

> was the one I wanted to spend my life with. Evidently he felt the same, because <u>about a month after this</u> realization hit me, he proposed. I'll always remember that day. It was <u>September 16th, 1959</u>. He was very romantic, taking me to a nice <u>restaurant in Atlanta</u>, and having the waiter serve the ring on a silver platter along with the dessert. We were married <u>8 months later</u>.

This covers all the information in the seven questions, but does so in a much more readable way. The narrative gets the questions themselves out of the way and lets the reader focus on the story. Here's another example of plain and simple writing.

> "We moved into our new house in 1965. Since we only lived in small apartments before, this seemed like a mansion. It had massive, old oak trees in the back yard, perfect for shading the picnic table and for hanging a swing from. I was soon busy planting flower beds and a small vegetable garden. The flowers brought us so much joy from spring through the fall, and the vegetables got us through some tough winters when Jim couldn't work his construction job.
>
> Billy was born while we lived here, in 1967. I loved decorating his room, even if we had to do so on a skimpy budget. But it forced me to be creative, and I think the room was better for it."

MIND MAPPING

Sometimes you might look at a topic and know you want to write about it, but not have any idea where to start. An easy way to get all the components of a topic down on paper is to do a "mind map." Start with a circle in the middle of a piece of paper, (See example in Appendix) write the topic in the middle of the circle. Then branch out from the circle with lines (think of a spider and its legs). On each line, write a sub-topic relating to the main topic. You can then branch off from the branches if needed. Once you've made a brief note of everything you can think of on this topic, go around the spider's legs and prioritize which you want to write first, second, etc. Then begin writing.

THE WRITER'S SIX QUESTIONS

As you're writing about your topic, keep in mind the six key questions used by journalists and writers for years:

>Who, What, Where, When, Why and How

Answer as many of them as apply to your story. However, don't try to go through the list and answer them in order, one by one, just try to incorporate the answers somewhere in your narrative. All the questions will probably not apply to every story, but at least go through them in your mind, and answer those that do apply. A sample outline guide to help you get all the information is shown in the Appendix.

BUILDING YOUR STORY

Construction

You will want to organize each story in a logical way. It should have a **beginning**, that sets the stage for what's to come, and gives as much background as necessary to explain what happens next.

Then you'll begin writing the **body**, which is the heart of the story. This is where you'll actually get into the plot, or the focus of your story, and describe all that happened and how you felt about it. This will add the "human-ness" to your story.

Finally, the **ending** should summarize, or draw a conclusion. You might tell what lessons were learned or how the experience changed your life. Remember, as you write your first draft, to allow enough spacing to add more details as you think of them. Then you can rewrite it later, if necessary.

Plot *(tells the What, Why and How)*

While we think of a plot as being integral to a mystery or adventure story, almost any story will have a plot – or a reason for being. Some stories may tell of conflict, or include action, and should have a definite outcome or resolution. Don't try to contrive a plot, but think about the reason for the story. Ask yourself – "what's the point of the story and why am I telling it." If there's no plot as such, make sure there is a point of some kind to the descriptions or conversations you're writing, even if it's only for its entertainment value. If there is an actual plot, use it to its full advantage.

Character Building *(tells Who)*

To make the people in your stories come alive for your readers, tell as much as you can about them; their physical attributes, backgrounds, education, vocations, personalities, strengths, weaknesses, mannerisms, habits, hobbies, etc. When possible, give examples of incidents that portray a "personality picture" of the person you're writing about. This will help your readers to better understand the characters, and why they acted the way they did. For example, *"Growing up during the depression caused him to be miserly as an adult."*

Setting the Stage *(tells Where and When)*

If the locale and environment of a story are important, make your readers see it as if they were there. Describe rooms, buildings, outdoor scenes, time of year, weather and anything else that would help the reader feel as though he's a part of it. In addition to describing the place, also describe the era, if it's relevant to the story. Was it during the depression of the Thirties, the war of the Forties, the "nifty Fifties," or the "psychedelic Sixties?" Tell as much as you can about the attitudes and concerns of society at that time.

LANGUAGE

You should write in a manner that's comfortable for you, or that includes words that are part of your environment. Don't worry about it being perfectly correct grammatically. If you're recounting a conversation in which someone uses the word *"Ya'll"* don't change it to *"All of you."* If your family has pet slang, use it, even if no one else does. The first time you use it, explain how the term came about, then continue to use it wherever applicable. A word that my grown children still use today is *"Char-char,"* which translates to cereal in our family. But when the kids were little and couldn't pronounce cereal, *char-char* is what they asked for, and it remains a pet term that we all still use. The same applies to names. Even though my sister's name was Andrea, we called her *"Tootie"* and that's how she is referred to in my stories. Let your personality come through in your writing. When those who know you read your stories, they should be able to "hear" you telling them.

To make your stories easier to read and more interesting, write in the active voice, rather than passive. For example: *"Hank milked the* cow" (active); not *"The cow was milked by Hank"* (passive.) When writing about yourself, write in the *first person* (as you would write a letter) rather than *third person* (as if writing about someone else.)

USING DIALOGUE

Whenever you can, use dialogue or conversations between people. You probably won't remember exact words, but try to convey the general message or meaning of what was said. You can generalize thoughts, words, and feelings to give an overview of what was happening without making up conversations.

For instance, in remembering a dog bite when I was small, (which explained my fear of dogs when I was younger) I initially wrote *"Mom yelled at the dog, then Grandma put a bandage on my arm and gave me a hug."*

After thinking about it, I remembered the general dialogue and rewrote it to read... *"Mom yelled 'Get away, get away' until the dog ran. Then Grandma bandaged my arm and gave me a big hug, and said 'It'll be okay, honey, Gram will make it better for you'."*

The dialogue adds more life and reality to the scene, and helps the reader to better visualize it. (This is not that important a story, but helps to explain the concept.)

Another way to add a person's words to a story is to use excerpts from actual letters to reinforce a point, add to a plot, or describe a relationship between two people. Excerpts also add to the authenticity of a story, since they are the actual words of the people involved.

SPEAKING OF AUTHENTICITY

Try to keep your story as authentic as possible. Verify whatever you can, and if you're not sure of some details, say so. Talk to others in the family, or old friends who were involved, to find out what they remember. Of course, you may find that they don't recall it at all the way you do. If you get different versions of a story, and can't get verification of either, write both sides and explain that the two of you remember two different versions. This is where some research will pay off. You're recording your history, and it will be in your family for generations to come. It's important to be as accurate as possible.

(See section on research for more information.)

ADDING DESCRIPTORS

Once you've answered the Who, What, Where, When, Why and How questions, and added as much other information as you can remember, begin to include more detailed descriptions. Look for places to use the senses, emotions, sizes, shapes and impressions. These will help bring your story to life, and add more impact for the reader. If you like, write the basic story first so you're not having to overthink it, then go back and add these extra descriptions.

If you're using a computer, you can easily go back and insert descriptors or make any other changes. Whether handwriting or typing, be sure to double space your first draft to allow room for changes when you reread it later.

The Senses

When adding descriptors, include the senses, such as **smell**, **sound**, **sight**, **taste** and **touch**. Try to include as much detail as you can, so the story won't be a sterile recitation of facts, but something the readers can see or feel as they read your words. But *do* write naturally. Don't use words or phrases that are so formal or flowery that you wouldn't use them in normal conversation. Remember, you're not trying to write a best-selling novel, you're just getting your life experiences documented for your family.

The Emotions

Next, work in your emotions. Were you happy, sad, terrified, proud, thrilled? Let the reader feel what you were feeling. Take care not to use the same words repeatedly. Look for variety. (See A Sampling of Descriptive Words)

The Rest

Finally, add other descriptors that give the reader a real sense of "being there." Describe or explain **textures**, **sizes**, **shapes**, **places**, and **impressions**. For instance – *"The tunnel was narrow with a low ceiling and jagged sides, making me feel trapped and frightened. The quiet darkness added to my claustrophobia, and the damp air sent a chill right through me."* The underlined words all paint a picture of the tunnel and how the person felt in it. It says a lot more than *"The tunnel was dark and I was scared."*

To add even more interest to your stories, when using conversations or dialogue from another person, include **quotes**, **humor**, and **ethnic** or **regional** language and pronunciations. When using descriptive words, use as much variety as you can. Instead of describing people as "nice," you could use words such as *gracious, kind, friendly, generous, charming, thoughtful, gentle*, etc. These words give a much better picture of a person than "*nice.*"

The same goes for the word "*pretty,*" whether describing a person, place or possession. Use words like *attractive, lovely, comely, gorgeous, delicate,* or *dazzling,* to give a more specific description.

To help you use more meaningful words, an example of alternate descriptors is included in the Appendix. A thesaurus is also helpful for finding just the right word to convey the meaning and feeling you're looking for.

Editing and Polishing

Once you've finished a story, put it in the appropriate section of the three ring binder. When you've completed the entire 28 days of work, you can go back and reread your stories. Try to read from the perspective of someone who doesn't know the story. See if there are any unanswered questions, inconsistencies, or areas that need to be edited for clarity. Make any changes necessary, and rewrite. You could also have someone else read it and make suggestions for improvement. This is where a writing group comes in handy; you can help each other make sure the story is as good as it can be.

If you haven't already done so, give each story a title. You won't necessarily have to use it when you compile the finished book, but it will help you identify the substance of the story in the meantime.

IMPORTANT

Begin each new story on a new page. That way, you can later put them in any order you wish, for continuity or consistency. You might want a story about a favorite pet to be included in the section on your childhood, or maybe you'd rather put it in a chapter about all the animals you've owned over the years. If you write each story separately, it'll be easy to rearrange later. If you're using a computer, this will be easy to cut and paste, anyway, but if you're writing longhand, it'll help you greatly to organize the final version.

Chapter 5

Day by Day Exercises

Each day of this plan has a specific exercise. It's best if you follow the sequence as laid out here, since the first few exercises lay the groundwork for later ones.

The first five days' exercises are to get all the vital information in one place. You may need to dig out some papers, or ask questions of other relatives to get information. Get as much as you can, but do not postpone moving forward until you have everything. Just keep going with what information you have, and try to fill in the blanks later.

On the sixth day, you will begin writing character descriptions or stories about people.

The following three weeks will be devoted to writing stories and anecdotes about specific events or periods of your life. There are a couple of exercises in which you will add to your list of experiences.

The last chapters tell you how to put together all your stories, depending on what you want the final outcome to be. As you write, be giving some thought to who you want to share your stories with, what purpose you want them to serve, and how many copies you will want to make.

Plan to set aside an hour or two each day to work on your book. Some days may only take a few minutes, while others will take a couple of hours. Try to be consistent in doing something every day. Within 10 to 14 days, you'll see quite a bit of progress, and be motivated to continue. The first few days of any long-term commitment (and – come on – four weeks isn't really *that* long!) are the hardest. Once you've honored your own commitment and stuck to your scheduled writing times, you'll find you're looking forward to each new installment.

When you look at the various lists of topic questions, plus the topics you come up with on your own, you may think "I can't write about all that in 28 days!" You're right, you can't. But the questions are just to get you thinking in case you develop writer's block. To finish in 28 days, you'll just be recording the *highlights* of your life; those events and experiences that you feel are the *most important* to hand down to your descendants. Once the 28 days are over, you may decide to continue writing about more of the topics, and that's great!

As you look at the topic questions I've provided, you'll also notice that usually several can be combined to make a cohesive story. (As in the example I gave in Chapter 4.)

So don't feel overwhelmed; you only need to follow the instructions, and you'll have a wonderful overview of your life in less than a month. Just stick with it!

NOTE: *The days shown are simply a guideline. While it's quite easy to complete your book in 28 days if you follow the guidelines, it's also likely that you may need to skip a day or two here and there due to other obligations, illness, etc. Don't let that deter you. Just pick up where you left off, and keep going. If it takes you 35 days to finish instead of 28, well, the important thing is that you finished! Keep going, no matter how many days it actually takes you.*

Chapter 6

Week One

This week's exercises will be relatively easy, since you will be recording facts that you know: names, dates, places, and other data that won't require any real writing or creativity on your part. They do, however, form the basis of the weeks to come, and will help ease you into the writing part gradually.

If you run into a roadblock – can't remember a date, for instance – don't let it stop you. Continue on with what you know, and use one of the Notes pages to jot down what you need to look for later.

NOTES

DAY 1 – THE VITAL STATISTICS AND LIFE LIST

Today you have two assignments, but both are relatively easy, and both should be fun. The first should only take about 15 minutes, the second may take a little longer, and require more thinking than writing. Have fun!

> TODAY'S GOAL 1: Get down the details of your birth and immediate family

This will be a quick, easy exercise, to get you started on your journey. It will provide the critical details of your life, that someone wanting to do a genealogical search would need to know.

Using the following list as a guide, enter as much information as you know, and try to find out the rest. Whether you're using a computer or writing by hand, try and list this information on one page. Be sure to list the headings below, so readers will know what the dates, places and names refer to (for instance, Sister: Sallie May).

- My Name at birth
- Date of birth
- Place of birth
- Mother's name*, birthdate & birthplace
- Father's name, birthdate & birthplace
- Maternal Grandmother's name*, birthdate & birthplace
- Maternal Grandfather's name, birthdate & birthplace
- Paternal Grandmother's name*, birthdate & birthplace
- Paternal Grandfather's name, birthdate & birthplace
- Sister(s) name, birthdate & birthplace
- Brother(s) name, birthdate & birthplace

- *Include maiden names wherever known

If you know, also include information about who you were named for, or why your name was chosen.

Add as much other information as you know, for instance, the address of your first home (where you were born, or brought home from the hospital,) names of other relatives; aunts, uncles, great-grandparents, etc. Think of this section as the information that would be included in a genealogy chart.

> TODAY'S GOAL 2: Start your own Life List - 50 items minimum

Take a sheet of paper and begin brainstorming the experiences and events of your life. Don't stop to think about whether or not it's important enough to include in your book of stories at this point. If a person, place, thing or event comes to mind, write it down. You can decide later whether it's worth writing a story about. A list of your topics might include items such as:

- Dad teaching me to ride a bike
- My 10th birthday surprise party
- Mom's Blackberry pie
- Summer camp - falling into the creek
- High school - skipping school & getting caught
- Mr. Barnes - inspiring teacher
- The day I met (spouse)

You get the idea. I'm sure you will come up with many topics. If you don't have a list of at least 50, you're not trying! You don't have to write a story about every topic you list, but one thing might remind you of another. And you may combine several topics into one story.

Write at least 50 items on the list today, and then add to it whenever you think of something else!

(<u>Note:</u> *You'll be adding to this list as well as drawing from it during some of the future exercises.*)

Day 2 – Make a Time Line

TODAY'S GOAL: Create a time line of your life from birth to present

A time line will help you to put your life's stories in order. It will answer the questions, What did you do, When did you do it, and Where were you when it happened? Be sure and include historical events as well, to demonstrate your place in history.

See the sample form in the Appendix for how to record the events. This form is a guide, only; feel free to design your own, including more or fewer columns or different headings. You can either use lined notebook paper, or, if working on a computer, use a database program, or columns in a word-processing program.

NOTES

DAY 3 – PLACES YOU'VE LIVED / SCHOOLS ATTENDED

TODAY'S GOAL 1: List the places you've lived since childhood.

It's fun to look back on places we've lived, remembering certain rooms, or hiding places, or favorite play areas. Today, list as many as you can. You may not remember exact addresses, or dates that you lived there, but do the best you can.

At the very least, try and list the city or town you lived in, and a range of years, if possible. Even if you don't have the details, this information will help those who may want to trace their roots in the future.

Later in the book, you can write stories, or provide more details and anecdotes about some of these places and the memories they bring back. For now, just get down as many facts as you remember.

Use the following as a guide:

From (Mo/Yr)   To (Mo/Yr)   City/Town, ST   Address

TODAY'S GOAL 2: Create a list of all the schools you've attended

Some of us may have only attended one or two schools in our lifetime - others may have changed schools every year. Try to list them all, along with the city and state, and the years you were there. Don't worry if you can't remember them all, or aren't sure of the years. Just do the best you can and leave blanks where you need to. You'll be surprised – the more you get into writing other stories, the more the memories will come back to you. Or get on the internet and do some research to find the name of a school in a particular town.

But, remember, it's not critical that you list every one of them; we're just trying to get a good overview of your life. Don't get bogged down on details. Record what you know, then move on.

Use the following as a guide:

From (Mo/Yr)   To (Mo/Yr)   School Name   City/Town, ST

NOTES

Day 4 – Jobs Held

TODAY'S GOAL: List all the jobs you've held in your lifetime

Once we were out of school – or in some cases, while we were still in – we began working, or perhaps joined the military. Your very first job might have been baby-sitting, delivering newspapers, or working in the family business. Go ahead and list those, too, if they were important to you, or started you on your life's career.

List the years (as best as you remember), the company name, address – or at least the city and state, your position there, what you earned, and maybe what your duties were. (See the guide below) If you still have old resumes on hand, they might be of some help in remembering some of the details. But again, I'll stress, don't get bogged down in the details you can't remember.

If you remember some interesting or funny stories about your jobs, make notes on them, so you can turn the notes into stories later. Right now, just focus on the details.

From	To	Company/Address	My Title/Duties	Salary

NOTES

Day 5 – Achievements/ Accomplishments/What You're Proud Of

"Forget what people think of you. You're people; what do you think of you?"

Anonymous

(Pull from the life list you created on Day 1, and then add whatever else you think of to round out this category.)

TODAY'S GOAL: List the things you're proud of

Some of the items you list here may already be in your life list. But often, we tend to forget some of the events that just made us feel good at the time, whether it be winning an award, being recognized for an achievement, or accomplishing something that seemed overwhelming at the time.

And yet, those are the very things our descendants would love to know about us.

Some examples might be:

- Your poem was published in the school newsletter
- Having a letter to the editor published
- Helping to build a house for Habitat for Humanity
- Running/walking a marathon
- Serving on board of directors of an organization/ company
- Taking a long road trip alone
- Raising confident, responsible children

Remember, it doesn't need to be anything newsworthy, just something *you* feel particularly proud of achieving.

Later, you will have an opportunity to write about a couple of the topics you feel most proud of. For now, just list as many as you can think of, starting in childhood.

NOTES

Day 6 – About Your Parents

"The family is the nucleus of civilization"
                                                Will & Ariel Durant

TODAY'S GOAL: Write two character descriptions

Now the fun begins, and some real writing. Up until now, you've been doing mostly fill-in-the-blanks details. Now you can let your creativity flow. Don't be intimidated by this; it's the most fun of all!

Begin by writing at least two character descriptions; ideally, write about each of your parents. But if you didn't have both parents in your life while you were growing up, write about another important person in your life; perhaps a grandparent, aunt or uncle. Eventually, you'll want to write about *all* of the special people in your family, but for now, start with the two who were most influential during your growing-up years.

If you're not sure how to start, remember my earlier tip regarding writing about any personal event or experience in your life. Pretend you're writing a letter to a friend, telling them about it. In this case, tell them about this amazing person in your life, describing how they look, how they talk, their personality, character traits, and how you felt about them. Write at least one full page; two or three would be even better.

If you still have difficulty getting started, try this exercise:

"Mama was... (physical attributes: tall, heavy, petite, pretty, energetic, etc.)"

"She always... (character traits: worked hard, showed love, encouraged others, etc.)"

"The thing I loved best about her was..."

"Her favorite things were..."

"She really disliked..."

TOPIC QUESTIONS:

- Where were your parents born?
- If they moved away from their birthplace, when and why?
- How did they make a living?
- What were some challenges they faced?
- What successes did they have in life?
- Do you know any stories about your parents as children?
- What were some of the best/most difficult times you had together?

<u>Suggested Exercise</u>: *Write a description of each of your parents or two other family members who were influential in your life. Answer the topic questions above in addition to, or as part of, the character descriptions.*

NOTES

_____

_____

_____

_____

_____

_____

_____

_____

_____

Day 7 – About Your Grandparents

TODAY'S GOAL: Write at least two character descriptions

We all began life descended from four grandparents, but not everyone was fortunate enough to have known all four of them.

In this exercise, write a character description of each of the grandparents you knew well. Use the same tips and ideas from the previous exercise for this one.

If one or more of your grandparents was not in your life, write what you know, based on stories you heard from your parents. Include the dates and places of birth from the Day 1 exercise. Once you think about it, and perhaps do a mind-map (see chapter 4), you may discover you know more about them than you thought.

Below is a list of some of the things you might want to cover when writing about your grandparents, but try to get their personalities down first. Write at least one full page about each grandparent you remember.

Topic Questions - Extended Family

- Where were your grandparents born?
- If not in the United States, when did they arrive here?
- Why did they come here? Where did they settle?
- How did they make a living?
- How far back can you trace your ancestors?
- Do you know any stories about your grandparents as children?
- Were you close to your grandparents? Did they live nearby?
- Describe their personalities, likes, dislikes, hobbies, etc.
- What were some of the best times you had together?
- What were some of the saddest or more difficult times?
- Did they ever live with you?

Suggested Exercise: *Write a description of each of the grandparents you remember. Include answers to as many of the above Topic Questions as you can.*

NOTES

CHAPTER 7

Week Two

Now that you've had a taste of writing, you get a break. Today, you'll just create another list. You may have already included some memories in your earlier Life List, giving you a head start. You can refer to that list for the next exercise or start fresh, since the previous exercises may have shifted your brain into gear, helping you recall lots more events.

Based on the list you will create, you will then write two stories a day about the most outstanding memories of each era of your childhood. When I say "stories", I don't mean it necessarily has to be about one specific event.

You could write a general overview of what you remember from your preschool days; the house you lived in, games you played, people you loved, etc. In the school years sections, you can write about a typical day at school, describing the classroom and some of your school chums, and what you liked or disliked about school.

If you get stuck for ideas, review the general topics listed in each section.

NOTES

Day 8 – Childhood/School Days

"Childhood is where competition is a baseball game and responsibility is a paper route."

Erma Bombeck

(Pull from the Life List you created on Day 1, and then add whatever else you think of to round out this category.)

> TODAY'S GOAL: Make a list of as many childhood experiences as you can remember. Write about one or two of those experiences.

For most of us, when we think of our childhood, a flurry of images come to mind. Take a sheet of paper, and begin writing down everything that comes to mind relating to your childhood and school experiences. You might write such notes as:
- Swimming in the creek
- Helping Dad on the farm
- Watching Howdy Doody on TV
- Picnics at the beach
- My 10th birthday party

It can be a wide range of topics. There are no rules, because it's *your* memories you're writing about. Just let your brain go, and write down everything that comes to mind; don't decide now whether or not it's important enough. There will be some things that won't merit an entire story, but you may want to give it mention in just a sentence or two of another story. So go ahead and add it to the list. After you've prioritized, and mind-mapped, you can decide if a particular item needs to be written about at all.

If your mind is just blank, and you're having trouble thinking of topics, don't despair. On the next page is a list of general questions regarding childhood. Go over that list, and next to each item, jot a note about something in your own life the topic might remind you of. This can be the basis for your stories.

But before going to the following questions, try and write down your specific experiences first. You'll feel more emotional involvement in those, because the memories are already ingrained in you (or you wouldn't have written them down!) Use the question list below for adding to your own memories, or if you just can't think where to start.

Once you have a list of at least 30 or 40 topics, go through it and prioritize which you'd like to write about first. You might also put a symbol next to several that could be combined into one story. For instance if three of your topics are: seventh birthday, new puppy, and broken arm, you'd want to combine them if it happened that you broke your arm and received a new puppy on your seventh birthday. Put an "x" or a "*", or some symbol next to each of the three items, to remind you to combine them. Use different symbols for different groupings.

Topic Questions – Childhood

- What is your earliest memory? How old were you? Who else was there? Was it a good or bad experience?
- Did you have favorite toys?
- What games did you play? What were some favorite activities?
- Describe some special times with friends
- Where did you like to play: park, yard, playground, neighbor's yard?
- What were you afraid of?
- What did you look forward to?
- Tell about when you misbehaved. Were you caught? Were you punished?
- Did you have any hideaways where you liked to be alone?
- Tell about brothers and sisters. Did you fight, or get along well?
- Where did you live during this time? Describe your house or room.
- Did you like to read? What types of books?
- What was your favorite and / or least favorite food?
- Did you ever run away, or think about it?
- When were you the most scared, excited, happy or proud?

- Did you have chores you were responsible for?
- Did you receive an allowance?
- Did you ever stay overnight away from home and parents? Were you homesick?
- Did you think about what you wanted to be when you grew up?
- What were you like as a child; shy, fidgety, confident?
- What are some of your happiest memories?
- Did you have pets? Who was responsible for them?
- Tell about your birthdays (parties, special gifts, etc.)
- Tell about family trips and vacations during this time
- Tell about special occasions (weddings, reunions, other celebrations
- Do any family traditions or rituals stand out in your mind?
- Who were your best friends?
- Describe some special times with friends
- Do you remember any funny or interesting stories during this time?
- Where did you live during this time?
- Describe your house. Did you have your own room?
- What was the phone system like? What type of heating/cooling?
- What was the yard like? Did you have a swing or gym set?
- Was it in the city or country? Did your family own many acres?
- What was the neighborhood like? Did you like the neighbors?
- What was the best thing about your neighborhood? The worst?
- Was there wildlife around your neighborhood?
- Was there anything scary in or near your house?
- Where was the nearest big city to you? Did you go there often?
- What did your family do for entertainment?
- What were some other activities, trips, celebrations, events?

Dee Dees

- What were some popular (or children's) songs from this period?
- What were some fads or "crazes" during these years?
- What were the popular toys, movies, radio or TV shows?
- Were there any serious weather problems, hurricanes, etc.?
- What was happening in the world during these years?

NOTES

DAY 9 – CHILDHOOD: BIRTH TO 12 (OUTSIDE OF SCHOOL)

TODAY'S GOAL: Write two stories today about your early childhood

These early years provided the basis for who we became later in life. Most of our personality, as well as a good portion of our emotional stability is formed during our early years.

Using the list from yesterday (both your own memories, and the listed questions) try to record as much as you can that will give some insight into how you developed into the person you've become.

You may not have many memories of this period, but write what you remember, and ask others to fill in the blanks. Parents, brothers and sisters, aunts, uncles and cousins can all help with details.

If you have a long list of memories, begin with those you <u>most</u> want others to know about you. Then continue writing about other events until you run out of steam. That way, you'll have the important things down first.

Now... enjoy reliving your childhood!

<u>Suggested Assignment</u>: *Describe what you were like as a young child. It may seem difficult, but go to a quiet place, close your eyes and think back. Were you happy, spoiled, angry, shy, outgoing, friendly, etc. Write 1 page. Then write one or two more stories about events or periods from the childhood list that you feel most strongly about.*

NOTES

Day 10 – Special People

<u>TODAY'S GOAL:</u> Write one story each about a best friend and/or relative who influenced your childhood.

There were many people in our lives other than our parents, who also influenced us in some way. Perhaps an older sister helped raise all the younger siblings, or a favorite uncle mentored a fatherless boy.

Maybe it was our best friend who stood by us when no one else would, who made us feel special.

For this goal, try to focus on at least one, preferably two, people who had an impact on your life when you were a child. It need not have been a huge impact, and it need not even have been life-changing. Perhaps it was just someone who made you feel good about yourself in small ways.

Describe the person, how you knew them (relative, friend, neighbor, etc.) Explain what was special about them, and how they influenced you.

Note: *For this exercise, try to use examples outside of school. There will be an opportunity in the next exercises to write about special people from your school experiences.*

NOTES

Day 11 – Grade School

TODAY'S GOAL: Write two stories about events that stand out about grade school

Our years in grade school go a long way toward forming the person we become. Teachers, principals, and even classmates, all have an impact on our lives during these early years. For this exercise, you might want to choose stories that demonstrate the influence others in your school life had on you.

If a particular teacher made you feel good about yourself, that might be a topic you'd want to share with your family. Or if a classmate became a lifelong friend, write about how you met, your first feelings toward each other, and how the friendship endured the years.

Again, if you have particular memories that are special to you, write about those first. Use the included topics only if you can't think of anything from your own life. Of course, many of the listed topics can be woven into your own memories, such as the name of the school, activities, and special events.

Now, go back to school, and this time... enjoy it!

<u>Suggested exercise:</u> *Write about a person from grade school, adult or child, who impacted your life in some way.*

Topic Questions – Grade School (Grades 1 - 6)

Note: *Many of these questions will also apply to the period of Junior/Senior High School in the next sections. For those that apply, write the topics on a separate sheet of paper and make notes on what you want to say about them.*

- Name the first school you attended. Where was it? Describe the buildings and grounds
- What were the rooms and desks like?
- Do you remember your first day at school?
- Were you scared; did you cry?
- Was there a playground? What did you do during recess?
- Were there special days at school such as May Day, track days, etc.?

- Were you in holiday programs or plays?
- Did you participate in extracurricular school activities?
- Did you take field trips? Where did you go? Did your parents go?
- Were your parents involved with your school or PTA?
- Did you have assemblies? Were there guest speakers?
- Did you begin the day with a Pledge of Allegiance, Prayer, Song, etc.?
- Did you have "snow days" or other unexpected school closings?
- Did you have air raid drills?
- Did you buy savings stamps or savings bonds?
- What did you usually have for lunch? Did you bring it from home?
- Did you use a sack or have a lunch box? Describe the lunch box.
- How were you as a student? Did you enjoy school and do well?
- What were your favorite/least favorite, best/worst subjects?
- Did you have special achievements, awards, or activities?
- Was there a "bad kid" in your class or school?
- Did you ever get in trouble at school? What for? Were you punished?
- Tell about your teachers. Which did you like, dislike, and why?
- Did any teachers have a special effect on you?
- Who were your friends? Were they different people than your "home" friends?
- Have they remained friends throughout your life?
- Do you know where any school friends or teachers are now?
- Did you have to change schools during this time? Were you nervous about a new school?
- Tell about any interesting things that happened at school during these years.
- Was there any event that stands out in your mind during this time?

DAY 12 – TEEN YEARS

"Too young for love, too old for toys
Boys dream of cars, girls dream of boys"

Dee Dees

TODAY'S GOAL: Write two stories about events *outside* of school during your teen years

Our teen years could have been the best of times, or the worst of times, but they were never dull! They were the years when we were going through a transformation from childhood to adulthood.

There were times when we learned great lessons, and times when we fell on our faces; times of achievement and a feeling of being invincible, and times of our worst humiliations and lowest self-esteem.

Whatever your memories of these times, describe them in as much detail as you can. Tell about some of the difficult times you had coming of age, dating, working out problems with parents, and dealing with the opposite sex. Tell about experiences that taught you valuable lessons, and present them in a way that might help teenagers today learn from your mistakes.

Suggested Assignment: *Write about your first "crush." Include how you met, whether the feelings were returned, a typical date, and describe the person in detail. How and why did it end?*

Topic Questions – Teen years

- Where did you live during this time?
- Describe the house and neighborhood
- What were some special times for you?
- What was your favorite entertainment or pastime?
- What was your perception of yourself during this time?
- What were your career aspirations at this age?
- Did you follow through on your career desires?
- Did you have an after-school job? Describe it.
- Describe your first car. Who bought it?

- Who were your best friends? Did your parents approve of them?
- Was there a certain group of friends, or clique, you hung out with?
- Were you popular, part of the "in crowd?"
- Was there a favorite "hangout?"
- Tell about your first date.
- Who was your first crush? Were the feelings mutual?
- Did you date a lot, or just have one or two steadies over the years?
- Tell about some of your dates, romances.
- When and how did you learn about sex?
- Who were your heroes? Were they people you knew, or celebrities?
- How did you get along with your family during this time?
- Were you rebellious?
- Were there any special family events, gatherings, or celebrations?
- Were there any special birthday celebrations for the "big" years (13, 16)
- Was there TV, and did you watch a lot? What types of shows?
- What kind of music did you like?
- What musical groups and singers were popular?
- Who were your favorite entertainers?
- Did you enjoy reading? What types of books?
- Did you play a musical instrument, or have a talent of any kind?
- What did you do to relax or get away from it all?
- What were some popular movies and songs of the time?
- Describe the fashions of the day.
- What hairstyles were popular?
- What fads were "in?"
- What fun events did you attend: concerts, shows, sports, etc.?
- What was happening in the world during these years?
- What were some special times for you?
- Were there any other significant events during this time?

Day 13 – High School (Grades 7 - 12)

TODAY'S GOAL: Write two stories about events that happened around your school life

High school was a time of angst for many of us. We worried about being part of the "right" groups, or whether or not we were popular. Some of us had college on our minds, and agonized over whether or not we'd make it.

There were sports and clubs to be involved in, and friends to hang out with. We began dating, and may have found the love of our life during high school.

Suggested Exercise: *Write one story about what seemed most important to you during high school. Did you worry about family, dating, sports, college, career, or just making it through each day?*

Topic Questions – High School Years

- Where did you go to Junior High (or middle school?)
- What High School did you attend?
- Was it a large school? Were the classes large?
- How many classes did you have in a day?
- Were there different teachers for each class?
- Who were your favorite teachers? Least favorite? Why?
- Did any teachers inspire or motivate you in any particular way?
- What were your favorite subjects? In which did you excel?
- What kind of student were you?
- Did you participate in physical education or sports? Which ones?
- Did you have to take group showers after PE? Did that bother you?
- Did you ever skip school? Were you caught?
- Were you ever in trouble? For what reason?
- Did many students drive to school?

- If not, how did most get there? How did you?
- Tell about special school activities (homecomings, senior trips, etc.)
- What clubs, activities, organizations, were you involved in?
- Did you receive any honors or awards?
- Did you attend pep rallies, football games, etc?
- Who were the most popular kids at school? What became of them?
- Did you go to Proms? With whom? Tell about your date.
- Did you graduate? Tell about the graduation ceremony.
- If you didn't graduate, what caused you to leave school?
- What was your school mascot, and school colors?
- Was there a school song or class song? Do you remember it?

NOTES

_____

_____

_____

_____

_____

_____

_____

_____

Day 14 – College/Advanced schools

*"We soon leave the nest for our solo flight,
To begin life anew, and set the world right."*

Dee Dees

TODAY'S GOAL: Write about your choice to either go or not go to college

If you attended college or any kind of vocational or advanced training schools, write two stories about the most memorable events of those times. It might be your first day, graduation, or perhaps a particular challenge or success you experienced while there.

If you did not attend any of these, write about why you did not. Was it your choice to not go, could you not afford it, did you have other obligations? Write about what you feel you missed, if anything, or what you feel you gained by going the route you did. Write what you would recommend your descendants and other youngsters do.

Below are some topics you might cover for each scenario.

Topic Questions: Advanced schooling

- Why did you choose the college or school you chose?
- What years did you attend?
- What classes did you enjoy most?
- What was your major and why did you choose it?
- Were you on a scholarship? What kind?
- Tell about awards/honors you received.
- Where did you live (campus, home, on own, etc.)
- Describe your roommates, and how you got along.
- What year did you graduate? Who attended?
- Were there any significant events during these years?

Topic Questions: No advanced schooling

- How old were you when you first left home?
- What were the circumstances of your leaving to go on your own?
- Where was your first home away from home?
- Describe the neighborhood.
- What was the most difficult part of living on your own?
- Did you cook your own meals? What were your favorites?
- Did you have roommates? Describe them.
- What were some problems you encountered?
- What are some fun memories of this period.

NOTES

_____
_____
_____
_____
_____
_____
_____
_____
_____
_____

Chapter 8

Week Three

You're halfway there! Whether you've actually come this far in only 14 days, or if it's taken you a bit longer, you've accomplished quite a bit. Be proud of what you've created, and continue on. It is hoped that you're enjoying the experience of looking back on your life's experiences and achievements.

We go through so many changes in our lives during our early adult years. Marriage, career, family, new homes, raising teenagers, and other challenges and successes along the way. Sometimes it's smooth sailing; other times it seems we'll never get through it.

This week you'll be focusing on careers and family. If you've married and had children, this is where you get to brag on your wonderful spouse, boast of your terrific children, and describe family vacations and special experiences while the children were growing up. If your spouse and children weren't the greatest, you'll still have some stories to tell about how you handled the difficult times.

As with last week, you'll begin the week by making a list. The following days you will write about specific events. Some exercises will be suggested, or you may choose to write about some of the topics from the list you created. Try for at least two stories (or one longer one that encompasses several events/periods.) Remember that you can always come back to the topic lists and write more stories later. The goal now is to have a comprehensive overview of the most *important* aspects of your life done in 28 days.

NOTES

Day 15 – Career and Family

(Pull from the life list you created on Day 1, and then add whatever else you think of to round out this category.)

> TODAY'S GOAL: Make a list of events related to your careers or family life. Write a story about a significant event during this time.

When creating your list for this week's goals and exercises, think about the highlights of your adult life: the birth of your children, promotions at work, places you've traveled, celebrations, times spent with friends, etc. Be specific when creating your list. You might write things such as:

- The day I met (spouse)
- Experiencing our first pregnancy
- Changing jobs - moving up in the business world
- Our Disneyland vacation
- Our first trip to Europe
- The day our youngest left home for college
- My best birthday surprise

Remember, you probably won't write about every single thing you list, but go ahead and list as much as you recall, simply because one thing will remind you of another. And you can weave several of the less important topics into one longer story.

NOTES

Day 16 – First job / Military

"The world is full of willing people; some willing to work, and rest willing to let them."

Robert Frost

Today's Goal: Write two stories about events in your working life.

A reality of adulthood is that we begin a career, or a series of jobs and careers. Some make the military a career, some try it out, others are never a part of it. For some of us, keeping a home and raising children is our career.

Most of us begin either not knowing what we want to do with our lives, or thinking we know, and then changing careers somewhere along the line. Others know from childhood exactly what they want to do, and end up doing exactly that.

Whether you were a career person, a soldier, or a keeper of the home fires, you worked hard and did your best. You learned a lot along the way. Share those lessons here.

Suggested exercise 1: *Write about your very first paid job.*

Suggested exercise 2: *Write about how you chose your lifelong career*

Topic Questions – Military
- Why did you go into the service?
- What branch (Army, Navy, etc.) did you choose, and why?
- Was there a war on at the time? Which one?
- If you were drafted, describe how you felt upon getting the notice.
- Was it hard for you to leave home?
- Did you leave a sweetheart back home?
- Did you go overseas?

- Tell about promotions, special awards, honors and recognition
- What was the highest rank you achieved?
- When were you discharged?

Topic Questions – Military Spouse

- Describe what it was like, being the one to stay at home, if you did.
- If he/she fought in a war, how did you handle the worry?
- Did you have the support of family while your spouse was gone?
- Did your spouse make a career of the military? Why / why not?
- How did you handle moving every few years?
- What did your children think of being a military family?

Topic Questions – Careers

Note: *You will already have recorded some of this info on Day 6. This is the place to tell the stories that go along with the data.*

You can apply some of these questions to all your jobs, either within the same company, or with different companies.

- Where was your first full time job?
- What was your title and occupation on your first job?
- How did you get the job, or get started in your career?
- How much did you earn when you began?
- Tell about raises, promotions, and special recognition.
- Did you travel as part of your job? Where did you go?
- What did you enjoy most about the job? What did you like the least?
- Why did you choose your profession?

Day 17 – How you met your spouse - Courtship - Wedding

Today's Goal: Write about meeting and dating your spouse, and about your marriage. If you've stayed single, write about that experience.

Most of us can remember (usually with fondness) how we met our mate. We know the place, the circumstances, and usually, the exact date. We often remember who else was there, and our first impressions of our future spouse. These are the stories our children and grandchildren delight in hearing.

This is the day to plan a little extra time, so you can do the exercise justice. Try to incorporate as much of the Who, What, Where, When, Why and How, as you can, as well as the senses. Tell how you felt, how he/she looked, whether or not there was music playing, whether it was raining, a sunny day, or nighttime. Describe this event in as much detail as you possibly can. The more detail you can add, the more real – and more interesting to read – it will be for future generations.

Of course, you can always come back and revise and add more later, if you wish. But try to get as much down as you can today. This exercise may be several pages long, but it will be worth it.

Note: *If you've been married more than once, you can do the same for each marriage, or if one turned out badly, feel free to gloss over the details, perhaps just telling how you met, what attracted you to the other person, and what went wrong.*

Suggested Assignment 1: *Write, in detail, how, where and when you met your spouse, and what your first impression was. Also include how long you dated before becoming engaged, what the proposal was like, and a bit about your wedding.*

OR...

Dee Dees

<u>Suggested Assignment 2:</u> *Write about why you remained single, whether it was by choice or circumstance.*

Topic Questions: Courtship and Marriage

- How did you meet your spouse?
- What was your first impression?
- Describe your courtship.
- When did you know this was "the one?"
- How long did you date before becoming engaged?
- Describe your proposal; where, when, and your memories of it.
- How long was your engagement?
- Were there engagement or bridal showers?
- Who held the showers? Who attended?
- What were some of the gifts you received?
- Were there bachelor parties? Describe them?
- What was your wedding like? Who were the attendants?
- Where was the wedding held?
- Where did you honeymoon?
- Describe the location and special memories.

NOTES

_____

_____

_____

_____

_____

_____

Day 18 – Early Family Life - Before Children

"A family is made of those we love, and those who love us, too. Whether they be kin or special friend, the bond we feel is true."
Dee Dees

TODAY'S GOAL: Write about several events from your life before children.

If we were fortunate enough to have a few years before children came along, we still had an adjustment period to go through. Getting used to each other, making decisions together, compromising when necessary, and handling difficult times.

Sometimes other family members; parents, in-laws, etc. were involved. Maybe we lived with them, or they lived with us.

Suggested exercise 1: *Write about your adjustment to married life*

Suggested exercise 2: *Describe your first home as a couple*

Topic Questions - Early Family Life - before children
- Tell about your first meeting with your in-laws to be.
- What was your first impression of them? Has it changed?
- Do/did you get along with your in-laws?
- Do/did they live nearby?
- Were there family gatherings?
- Who were your friends?
- Tell about activities with friends.
- Did you take trips together?
- Describe any special events or memories of this period.
- Did you move to a different home during this time? Why?

NOTES

Day 19 – Children

You probably have lots to tell about your children, but remember, this is your story. Try to limit your writings about each to a general overview of their character, personality, and traits. You might tell what you love about them, or what has made you proudest.

Just remember to treat each of them equally, as they'll all be reading this at some point. If one child has a particular talent that the others lack, be sure and point out the strengths or skills of the others also.

For this exercise, you can write a general overview of family life as a whole, or write a page or two about each child. For ideas, refer to the list you created two days ago, or the earlier Life List. If you're still stuck, the topic questions below will provide some help.

<u>Exercise 1</u> - Complete the following information for each child

        Name   Birth date   Birthplace

<u>Exercise 2</u> - *Write a description of each of your offspring as a child. Describe their personalities, looks, likes and dislikes. Write at least one page per child.*

TOPICS: CHILDREN - GENERAL

- Describe the first pregnancy
  (men – discuss it from your point of view)
- Were there baby showers? Who gave them?
- What were some special gifts you received?
- Tell about the birth of your firstborn.
- Describe your feelings when you first saw your newborn.
- How did you adjust to the addition to the family?
- Was money tight during these years?
- Did both of you work? If so, who cared for the children?
- Where did you live during this time?
- Describe your house, yard and neighborhood.

- Where did the children like to play?
- Did you play games as a family?
- Tell about some family trips and vacations with small children.
- Tell about some highlights or special times as a family.
- How did you discipline your children? How did you reward them?
- Did you and your spouse agree on how to raise them?
- What do you wish you had done differently with them?
- Did you start any new family traditions?
- Did you and your spouse have opposing traditions?
- How did you resolve them?

Topic Questions - Children - specific (if writing about each child individually, answer some of these questions)

- Why did you choose their name?
- Was there a nickname? How did they get it?
- Describe his/her personality, talents, strengths, weaknesses
- Describe some accomplishments and achievements
- Where did he/she start school? What year?
- What kind of student was he/she?
- When did they leave home? Why, and where did they go?
- What were his/her goals? Have any been achieved?
- If married, to whom?

Day 20 – Special Occasions

"Enjoy the little things, for one day you may look back and realize they were the big things."

Robert Brault

Today's Goal: Write about one or two special times in your life (not already covered earlier)

We sometimes think of special occasions as "dress up" times; weddings, graduations, parties, and so on. But a special occasion can be any time that holds special memories for you. It could be the camping trip by the lake, a surprise birthday party, or winning an award.

We usually remember the event in general, but this section will give you an opportunity to think about and record the details; not just what happened, but also how you felt about it. Special occasions are often times of high emotion. Now you can describe those emotions, and let your readers know exactly how much the event meant to you.

Suggested Exercise – *Describe the best surprise you've ever had*

Topic Questions: Special Occasions

- Did your family celebrate "little victories" (good report card, first job, winning the spelling bee, etc.)
- What holiday do you enjoy the most? How do you celebrate it?
- Do you have any unique holiday traditions?
- Do you usually get together with extended family for holidays?
- Have you ever had a surprise Birthday or Anniversary party?
- Do you remember your confirmation or baptism?
- Have you ever attended a high school or college reunion?
- Have you ever reunited with someone after many years apart?

NOTES

Day 21 – Proudest Achievements

Today's Goal: From the list you created on Day 5, describe some of the achievements you're most proud of. Write at least a paragraph about as many as you can.

In case you're having trouble remembering some of your accomplishments, maybe some of the following categories will help you.

- Artistic (Writing, painting, drawing, sculpting, etc)
- Talent (Musical, Drama, Dance, Humor)
- Sports
- Volunteering
- Travel
- Media (TV / radio appearances, Newspaper / magazine coverage)
- Leadership
- Career-related
- Family-related
- Community-related

NOTES

CHAPTER 9

Week Four

DAY 22 – TRAVELS: HIGHLIGHTS OF PLACES YOU'VE VISITED

Today's Goal: Describe one or more of your trips/vacations

Where are some of your favorite places? What were some of the highlights of those trips? Where would you like to go back to? Where would you like to go that you have not yet been?

Begin by making a list of all the U.S. cities you've visited, as well as all cities/countries outside of the U.S. Add the dates (or at least the year) you were there.

We all have our favorite vacation spots. Think about how you would describe yours to someone who had never been there. Write about it, including why you chose to go there, what the best experience was, who was with you, how long you stayed, and anything else that is unique to your trip.

TOPIC QUESTIONS - TRAVEL

- How did you spend summer vacations as a child?
- Did your family go on trips, or did you stay around home?

Dee Dees

- Did you ever take a "spring break" trip as a high school or college student?
- What was the first trip you ever took alone? Did you enjoy it or feel lonesome?
- Do you like busy vacations or relaxing ones?
- Did you ever go camping? Where?
- Did you "rough it" or go in style with a manufactured camper?
- Where in the U.S. have you enjoyed visiting the most?
- Have you traveled overseas?
- What did you enjoy the most?
- Is there any country you would like to return to?
- What place have you always wanted to visit, but haven't?
- Where are some of the prettiest, most interesting or most exotic places you've visited?
- Have you ever traveled by train? By bus? Did you enjoy it?
- Do you remember your first airline flight?
- Have you had any unusual adventures while traveling?

NOTES

_____

_____

_____

_____

_____

_____

Day 23 – Clubs/Organizations/ Civic involvement/Volunteerism

"The smallest of deeds done is better than the greatest of intentions."

Unknown

Today's Goal: Describe your involvement in a group or organization that has been most meaningful to you.

Most of us at one time or another become joiners. Whether it be Lions, Soroptomist, PTAs, political parties, or the local homeowners association, there's always some group that needs our help and our skills. Or we may join a group that benefits us in some way, such as Toastmasters, a networking group, or a self-improvement group. Some of us join lots of different groups in our lifetime; others join one and get very involved in it.

List some of the organizations you've belonged to. Why did you join, what were your goals, what did you get out of the experience, did you hold leadership positions? Discuss civic involvement and volunteer positions you've held. Why did you get involved in each? How did the experience affect you?

Suggested Assignment 1: *List all the organizations you have belonged to.*

Suggested Assignment 2: *Write about the one or two you feel gave you the most satisfaction.*

Suggested Assignment 3: *Describe something you accomplished as an adult that took effort and persistence on your part. Did you think you could do it? Did you plan and work towards it for years, or did it just come about out of necessity? Did you have support, or did others scoff? What did you learn from the experience? Did your self-confidence and self-esteem grow?*

Topic Questions: Community Involvement

- Name some of the organizations you have belonged to.
- Tell what the purpose of each group was.
- Why did you want to be a part of it?
- What was accomplished while you were there?
- How did you benefit from membership or participation?
- Did you hold any offices? What was the highest office held?
- Have you been asked to be a leader of a group or committee?
- Were you able to motivate others while in your leadership roles?
- Have you been involved in church or synagogue committees?
- Would you rather be a leader or a follower?
- Have you ever spearheaded a committee for a cause you believed in?
- Have you ever served on jury duty?
- What did you think of the experience?
- In what political party are you registered?
- Do you always vote party lines, or the way your family always did?
- Have you ever run for or been elected to a political office?

NOTES

_____

_____

_____

_____

Day 24 – Retirement and Grandchildren

Today's Goal: Write an overview of where you are in this point of your life

If you have retired, you'll have a whole new aspect of your life to write about. You can tell about how you've adjusted to it (or how you've adjusted to your spouse's retirement!) how you spend your time, whether or not you've traveled, and where.

If you have grandchildren, or even great-grandchildren or beyond, describe each one, and explain what they have brought to your life.

You may not have reached retirement age yet, nor have grandchildren. If not, you probably have plans and dreams for your life after retirement. Write about those. Where do you see yourself five or ten years from now; what do you want to be doing; where do you think you'll live, and how will you support yourself?

By writing it down, if you have not done so before, you'll help clarify what you really want in life, and it may even help you to better plan for it.

If you don't have grandchildren yet, make some notes about what you would wish for them, what words of advice you would give, etc. At some point after they begin coming along, you may want to turn those notes into a letter for each one of them.

Suggested Exercise: *Write about your life today, whether retired or not.*

Suggested Exercise: *Make notes of things you want to tell your grandchildren, whether they're here yet or not.*

Topic Questions: Retirement
- When did you retire? Was there a ceremony?
- How long did you stay with your last employer? Was it fulfilling?
- Has your spouse retired?
- Did you have difficulty adjusting to retirement (or your spouse's)

- How do you spend your leisure time?
- Have you been able to travel? Where do you prefer to go?
- Are you a "snowbird" or a "summer person"?
- Are you involved in any volunteer activities?
- Do you belong to any retiree clubs, groups or organizations?
- What hobbies do you have?
- Have you learned any new hobbies, crafts or skills since retiring?
- Are you computer literate and on the internet?
- Has this opened up a new world? Or are you fighting the technology?
- Are you as financially stable as you had hoped you'd be at this time?
- What do you wish you had done differently about planning for retirement?
- Tell about any significant events during this period.

TOPIC QUESTIONS: GRANDCHILDREN

- For each, tell their full name, date and place of birth, and who their parents are.
- When did you see your first grandchild?
- What were your feelings at the time?
- How many do you have now? Any great-grandchildren?
- Were you able to see them often when they were growing up?
- What do they call you?
- Do you have pet names for them?
- Did/do they spend time at your home (sleep overs, vacations, etc.?)
- What activities did/do you enjoy doing with them?
- Tell what makes each one special.
- What advice would you give to your grandchildren?

Day 25 – Reflections

"For all sad words of tongue and pen, the saddest are these: 'It might have been'"

John Greenleaf Whittier

TODAY'S GOAL: Choose one of the topics most meaningful to you, and write two or three pages about it.

"If I had my life to live over..." We've probably all said that at some time or another. Would we choose a different career? Marry a different person? Live somewhere else? Travel more? Worry less?

Today's topic explores those questions, as well as your ideas about the kind of person you are, what you wish for your family, and other thought provoking issues.

Take your time with these topics. Give them lots of thought, and say what's really in your heart. Branch out beyond the questions listed and share your thoughts on the world, the nation, politics, society, values, and anything else you'd like to get off your chest. This is the most personal of all the daily assignments. Make it truly your reflections on your life.

You have a lifetime of wisdom to share. This is the place to begin.

<u>Suggested Assignment</u>: *Tell of a choice you made that determined a part of your future. If you had made a different choice, how would your life have been different?*

Topic Questions: Second Thoughts
- If you had your life to live over, what would you do differently?
- Have you reached the goals you set for yourself?
- Will you? If not, why not?
- Do you have any regrets about choices you've made in life?
- Any regrets about actions you've taken or not taken?

- Was there a different career you always thought you would like?
- Where would you have lived if you had it to do over?

Topic Questions: Lessons Learned

- Tell about trying something new, especially if it was scary or challenging?
- Describe some obstacles you've had to overcome, or challenges you've taken on.
- How did they affect you?
- Did you ever take a leap of faith, involving risk or adventure?
- What was the outcome? What did you learn from it?
- Tell about mistakes you've made from which you've learned.
- What is one of the best lessons you've learned in life?

Topic Questions: Changes

- Describe some of the changes you've seen in your lifetime.
- What are some historical/technological changes you've seen?
- Describe some of the political, national or world events you've seen.
- How did they affect you emotionally, if at all?
- Were there any world or national events that changed your life?

Topic Questions: Wisdom and Insight

- What words of wisdom have been passed on to you?
- What would you pass on to others?
- What types of things have scared or worried you the most?
- Were any of them legitimate worries?
- What do you feel are your strengths?
- What do you see as your weaknesses?
- What were some milestones that caused change in you, or caused your life to take a different turn?
- How would you want people to remember you?

Topic Questions: This 'n' That

- What are some of your proudest moments?
- What were some of the most exciting times in your life?
- Have you had your "15 minutes of fame"? What was involved?
- How did you react to your milestone birthdays (30, 40, etc.)
- What are your achievements and successes in life *outside* of work?
- Tell about some of your lifelong (or longtime) friends, or special people in your life.
- How did you meet, why were you close, and where are they now?
- What family traditions would you like to see carried on?

NOTES

Day 26 – The World Around You

"None of the questions that bother us today have an easy answer, and many of them have no answer at all."
                                                            Dwight D. Eisenhower

Today's Goal: Pick an era that impacted you the most and write about those times.

So much goes on in the world that we have little or no control over, yet affects us in some way or another. You've seen a lot of world changes in your lifetime – some good, some not. This is an opportunity for you to vent your feelings about some of the things you've seen. Tell how you feel about our leaders, our political system, and the various "movements" that have come and gone over the years.

This section gives you even more opportunities to record your feelings, beliefs, and perceptions, rather than just relating facts. Use the skills you've practiced in the previous assignments and let it all out. And if you can pass along any insights gleaned along the way, by all means, do so. You may be advising a future leader of our country.

While today's topic may seem like a lot of work at first glance, remember, you don't have to cover *everything* listed. Just choose one or two events or questions that impacted you personally, and address those.

Remember, this is *your* life story, and should include some of your impressions of the world you lived in, but does not need to touch on every single thing that happened.

Suggested assignment: *Write about the Sixties as you lived them. Describe the clothes, music, news events, subcultures, political upheavals, changes in morals, riots, etc. and their impact on you or your family, if any.*

Dee Dees

TOPIC QUESTIONS: THE WORLD AROUND YOU

- Express your thoughts, opinions or feelings about some of the following events:
    - The Depression
    - World War II
    - The Korean War
    - The Vietnam War
    - Watergate
    - The Space Program and Moon Landing
    - September 11th Attack
- What do you wish the federal government would change?
- Have you voted in most elections?
- Do you think government should be more – or less involved in our lives? Give some examples.
- Have you ever wished you were in charge?
- What would you do differently?
- Do you participate in local government? Attend council meetings?
- Who was your favorite / least favorite president, and why?
- Who are some statesmen you have admired and why?
- How do you feel about changes in morality over the last 40 years?
- How much do you feel movies and TV are to blame for those changes?
- Were you ever part of the Beatnik, Hippie or any other "movement"
- Did you feel threatened by these types of groups?
- Would you say you're a liberal, conservative, or a bit of both?
- How involved do you think we should be in affairs of other nations?
- Under what circumstances should we definitely intervene?
- When should we stay out?
- What do you think of our justice system? Is it the best for the most?

Day 27 – Catch-up Day / Where Are They Now?

Today's Goal 1: Catch up and/or tell us more about people mentioned earlier.

In doing the previous assignments, you probably thought of lots more experiences to write about than you had time or room for. Today will allow you to write about any of those; work, family, children, trips, celebrations, struggles, etc.

Remember to choose the things you think are the *most important right now* for you to get down on paper. You can always add more once the 28 days are up.

Where are they?

Oftentimes we lose track of people who were once important to us. It's a sad fact of life that everyone moves around much more than was done fifty, sixty or seventy years ago, and it's easy to lose touch. On the other hand, the internet makes it easier to stay in touch, if we know where a person is.

Write a bit about some of the people you've mentioned in earlier stories, and if you didn't already do so, tell what happened to them. Are they still living? Where? Do you still communicate? Or have you lost track completely of them?

This may even spur you on to try and find some of those individuals you've lost touch with over the years. If you do find them, tell them what they meant to you and how they touched your life. You might just make someone's day!

Suggested exercise 1: *Write a story or two about experiences that you haven't had a chance to record before now.*

Suggested exercise 2: *Write a paragraph or so about each of the characters who played a big part in your life, telling what happened to them and where they are now.*

NOTES

Day 28 – Letter(s) to Loved Ones

Today's Goal: Write a letter of love and appreciation to your family.

Now, this will take some thought. There are two ways you can do this.

1) You can write a letter to all your loved ones as a group, telling them what they've meant to you as a family, and how they've brought joy to your life. You could address each by name, and spend a paragraph or two talking to each individually.

2) You could write individual letters to each one, which will probably take longer, depending on the number of letters you choose to write. If you decide to do this, you may want to spread it out over the course of the day, taking a break between each letter, and thinking about what you want to say in the next one.

Some things to include are:

- How you feel about them
- What they've brought to your life
- What you wish for their future
- Words of advice

Writing these letters can sometimes become emotional, so get yourself in a good state of mind, find a quiet place where you won't be interrupted, and just do it.

If you've been writing your stories on a computer, you might want to hand write the letters. You can always transfer them to the computer if you want them included in your book, but it's still nice for each individual to have their own handwritten copy. (Or you can use the computer first, to make editing easier, and copy it in your own hand later.)

Try and finish the letters to spouse and children today, and you'll be done with the writing part of your book. If you want to add more letters to grandchildren, siblings, or other special people in your life at a later time, you'll always have that option (but do it sooner, rather than later).

<u>Today's assignment</u>: *Complete either option 1) or 2) above.*

NOTES

Chapter 10

Fun stuff

"It's the 'stuff' we keep and treasure, that tells us who we are."

Dee Dees

You've completed the last assignment. Congratulations! If you've come this far, you've done more than most people ever do. Whether you actually achieved it in 28 days is immaterial. The point is, you did it!

If you like, you can go directly to the next chapter, decide how you want to finish your book, and be done. It can be as simple as printing out the pages from your computer, putting them in a three-ring binder, and that's it!

Or... you can add a few more things, that require little writing, but that will add more of your personality to the finished product. If you'd like to do that, this chapter is for you. Here are some extras you can add.

PHOTOGRAPHS:

Any photos you have in your computer can easily be printed out for use in your book. But even for older pictures (pre-digital age) it's quite easy now to get good copies of either color or black and white photos. Be sure to write a caption identifying the people, places, dates, and events.

KEEPSAKES:

Make copies, (reduce if necessary) of awards, certificates, letters, recognition, newspaper mention, etc., that relate to events in your life.

POEMS, WRITINGS:

If you write, include some of your own work; essays or poetry, for instance. Explain why you wrote it and its meaning to you.

RECIPES:

Include some treasured family recipes. Make notes about where you got the recipe, and some special occasions where they were served.

SCRIPTURE, QUOTES, VERSES, MOTIVATORS, JOKES:

Include some of your favorites. You could group them all on a page or two, or perhaps use them as chapter headings. Be creative.

LIST OF FIRSTS:

Special "firsts" that haven't been included elsewhere: First kiss, first roller coaster ride, first time driving a car, etc.

WHERE WERE YOU WHEN:

Pearl Harbor was hit, Kennedy was shot, man landed on the moon, you first learned of the 9/11 attack, and other big news items. Tell the where, when, and especially your reaction to the event.

CLOSE ENCOUNTERS:

Have you ever met a celebrity? Tell who, the circumstances, and your reaction.

THE WAY IT WAS IN... :

Novelty or card shops, or scrapbooking stores often carry forms or cards with information about individual years, that list significant events such as who was President, what movie won the Oscar, what was happening in the world, and the price of bread, a house, or a new car. Use the information when talking about particular years.

Collages:

Make a couple of pages of collage, using old photos, advertisements, headlines, quotes, etc., to depict a certain era. Include prices of items during that time. Old National Geographics are a good source for ads and prices. The internet should yield quite a bit of information about a particular year or decade.

Memory Sketch:

Draw a sketch of the house you lived in as a child, your neighborhood, or your room. Or sketch anything that is difficult to describe in words. It doesn't have to be a perfect drawing, just a simple sketch to give the reader a general idea of what you're describing.

Family Tree:

Create a simple family tree going back as far as you can. List as many names of grandparents, great-grandparents, as you know, along with birth dates and places if you know them. Check any book on genealogy if you're not sure how to chart it out, or go on the internet.

Favorite Things:

List your favorites in categories that are meaningful to you. For instance, you might list your favorite Color, Flower, Jewel, Song, Book, Movie, Entertainer, Hobby, Way to Relax, City, or Vacation Spot.

Chapter 11

Finishing Touches

> *"A long life may not be good enough, but a good life is long enough"*
>
> Benjamin Franklin

You now have pages and pages of your stories, you've added those extra touches that make the book uniquely yours, you've accumulated the photos and other memorabilia you want to include – now, what do you do with it all? How do you get it into a format that you can duplicate and give to your family and friends?

This chapter will cover your options. Whatever method you choose, have fun with it, and be proud that you have truly created a legacy for your heirs; the legacy of a lifetime... *your* lifetime!

Editing:

Before you do anything more, read over all your stories, and do whatever editing is necessary. Clean up the grammar, correct the punctuation and spelling, and make sure your sentences make sense.

Transcription: (optional)

If you've handwritten all your stories, have someone else read them over for legibility. If they had no trouble reading your handwriting, you can use them as is. If they did have difficulty, or if you just want a more professional look, consider having someone type your stories.

You might find a friend or relative to do it for you, or you might hire a professional. They will also do editing for you, if you wish. Check the phone book or internet for "Transcribers," "Typists," or "Word Processing." Be sure you have a signed agreement as to how they charge, and an estimate for the services for your project.

ORGANIZING CHAPTERS:

If you followed the suggested outline for your tabbed dividers, you only need put the stories and additional information in the appropriate chapters, and you're organized. Sometimes, though you may want to rearrange a few stories, in a way that is more logical.

You might also want to add a couple of extra chapters, to further break the stories down in a way that makes it flow better. Don't feel constricted by the guidelines in this book. Make it *your* book, and organize it any way that works and makes it cohesive.

CHAPTER TITLES:

Once you have your chapters organized, read through and decide on a title for each one. It could be as simple as "Childhood", "Teen Years", etc. or you could come up with something more catchy and descriptive of the contents, such as "First Years in Arizona" or "Becoming Empty Nesters."

BOOK TITLE:

If there is a phrase that seems to sum up your life, it might be a good title for your book. Or if you have a favorite saying that you live by, try that as a title. Visit bookstores and the library and look at some autobiographies on the shelf for ideas.

If you really can't come up with anything clever, there's nothing wrong with "My Life by John Smith" or "The Life of Jane Brown"

TABLE OF CONTENTS:

It's a nice touch to have a Table of Contents at the front of the book, but by no means necessary. If your book becomes thick with future additions, it would be a good idea to use one.

INTRODUCTION:

If you want to relay a personal message to your readers as to why you wrote your book, and what you hope they will gain from it, an introduction is a good place to do so. Just a couple of paragraphs may be all you need to convey your message.

DEDICATION:

This, too, is strictly optional, and a nice touch if there's someone in your life you want to acknowledge as being special to you. It could be parents, spouse, children, friends, teachers, or all of the above. The dedication should go on a page by itself in the front of the book.

PRINTING:

Once you've got it the way you want it (don't worry about perfection, just so long as it's readable and coherent) decide how many copies you need. Below are several options:

1) One copy: You can keep it in the three-ring binder you've started using, and continue adding to it as you wish.

2) Several copies: Have all the pages copied at a quick print place such as Kinko's, Sir Speedy, AlphaGraphics, or one of the big office supply stores. Check around for prices per copy, including the number of photo pages you might have.

You can also have your books bound at these shops. Ask about prices for stapling, spiral binding, or plastic comb binding. Look at samples of each, so you'll have a good idea what you want.

It would be easiest to have the books be 8.5 x 11, since that's the size that will come out of your printer, or most likely the size notebook paper you'll be using if you hand write your stories.

You could also just use three-ring binders for the copies, if you like, as they're very inexpensive. If you do this, ask the quick-copy shops to punch holes in the copies for you.

An advantage of using the binders is that you can continue to add pages to each one as you continue to write, though you might be mailing out additional pages every so often.

The advantage to the bound copies is that it's more professional looking, and pages aren't likely to get lost.

3) Many copies: If you want more than 50 or 100, you may want to consider professional printing and binding. Contact print-on-demand businesses, who will print small runs. Compare the price per book with the price at the quick-copy shop, to see where a good break point would be. At some point, it will be cheaper to have 50 or 100 printed, than copied. You'll have to ask around to find the cutoff in your area.

If you choose this method, you'll probably want the smaller 6x9 size "trade paperback" size. That will involve some additional layout and formatting, either on your part or by someone else. If others handle it, there will be more cost involved. Be sure and ask about all this when talking to printers.

COVER DESIGN:

Having the books perfect bound presents you with another issue – cover design. You might want to get a professionally designed cover, but even a simple one will involve some expense. Talk to printers who do perfect bound books about their recommendations.

For options 1 and 2 above, it will be much simpler. You can design a cover on your computer, print it out on regular paper, and insert it in the clear plastic sleeve on the front of most binders.

For the wire bound or coil bound, print out your cover design on regular paper, and have the copy shop print it on card stock. Be sure and include a back cover (or just use blank card stock for the back.)

CHAPTER 12

The Next Step

So you're finished, right? Well, that's up to you. You worked hard this past 28 days, and you've got a book full of stories about your life, and maybe some pictures and fun things to add to it. If you accomplished what you wanted, then you're finished.

However, your life is still continuing. Who knows how many more adventures, travels, awards, or celebrations are still ahead?

Why not just think of the current stories as being "caught up." Now you can begin recording events as they happen.

Buy a journal, or at the very least a small notebook to carry around with you, and take notes on the big events in your life. No need to record every little thing, what you ate, where you went, every day of your life. But take notes on your next trip; what you saw, where you traveled, your feelings about it. Jot down the circumstances surrounding the surprise birthday party your kids gave you, or how you went parasailing for the very first time.

You always think you'll remember events, but time has a way of fading one's memories. Write it down. Then, when you have some spare time, go through your notes, and write out full accounts of the event. Add these new stories to your three-ring binder, and when you think you've got enough, compile them all into Volume II of your life's story!

Continue writing and adding stories, as long as you live, and you will leave your future generations a treasure worth having. While most other material things you pass down will probably be gone in a decade or two, the story of your life will be treasured from one generation to the next, for possibly hundreds of years.

You will not be just a name on a page, or a picture in a shoe box, but a person with a life well-lived. You'll be an individual who overcame challenges, enjoyed successes, and had opinions, wisdom and advice for generations to come. Only you can make it so. Go forth and write.

APPENDIX

YOUR TIMELINE

Mo/Yr	Event	In the News	I lived in...	President

Mo/Yr	Event	In the News	I lived in...	President

Mo/Yr	Event	In the News	I lived in...	President

Mo/Yr	Event	In the News	I lived in...	President

MIND MAPPING EXAMPLE

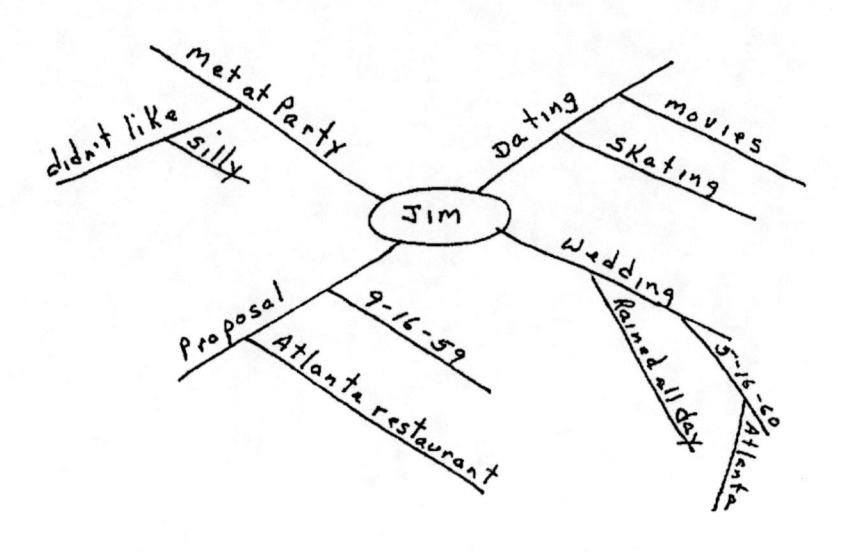

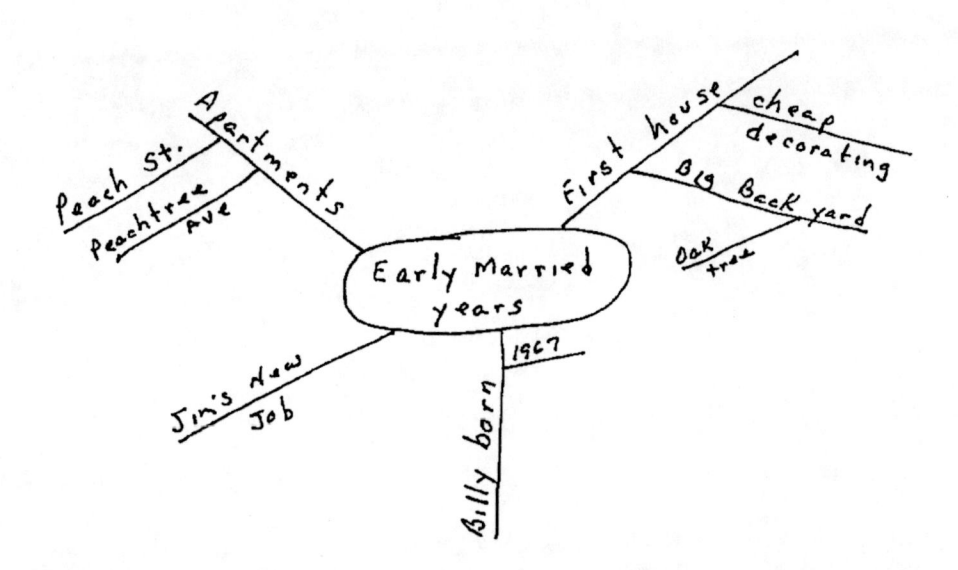

Jim
- Met at Party
  - didn't like
  - silly
- Dating
  - movies
  - skating
- Wedding
  - Rained all day
  - 5-16-60
  - Atlanta
- 9-16-59
- Proposal
  - Atlanta restaurant

Early Married Years
- Apartments
  - Peach St.
  - Peachtree Ave
- First house
  - cheap decorating
  - Big Back yard
  - Oak tree
- Jim's New Job
- Billy born
  - 1967

105

A SAMPLING OF DESCRIPTIVE WORDS

SENSES

Sight
beautiful
breathtaking
bright
dazzling
gorgeous
lovely
radiant
scenic
spectacular
frightful
grisly
homely
misshapen
plain
repulsive
unsightly

Sound
barely audible
bellow
boisterous
booming
grating
muffled
roar
rustling
silent
soothing
thud
tinkling
whisper

Taste
delectable
delicious
sour
sweet
tangy
tart

Touch
delicate
embrace
grasping
pat
pounding
squeezing
stroke
tender

Smell
aromatic
fragrant
odoriferous
pungent
putrid
scented
sour
stinky
sweet

EMOTIONS/ ATTITUDES
afraid
anticipating
anxious
awestruck
dejected
distraught
empathetic
excited
flabbergasted
imaginative
intimidated
judgmental
passionate
sympathetic
tactful
thrilled
understanding

PERSONALITY TRAITS
brave
cold-bloded
compassionate
dull
effervescent
forgetful
frugal
generous
gentle
graceful
hard-hearted
hateful
intellectual
loving
mean-spirited

miserly
nervous
reserved
sensible
sensitive
taciturn
tense
thoughtful
vivacious

SIZES

diminutive
enormous
extensive
gigantic
huge
mammoth
massive
miniature
monstrous
petite
tiny
vast
wee

TEXTURES

coarse
crinkled
glossy
grainy
gravelly
jagged
ridged
rough
ruffled
sharp
slick
smooth
soft
velvety
wrinkled

SHAPES

circular
cubic
multi-faceted
oblong
oval
rectangular
round
square

IMPRESSIONS

dainty
elegant
extravagant
magnificent
nerve-wracking
overpowering
peaceful
relaxing
still
tranquil

Also available...

LifeNotes – Recording your Memories... the Legacy of a Lifetime

LifeNotes is an 8.5 x 11 spiral bound workbook that explains how to record the stories of your life, and gives you the tools to get all your thoughts and memories down on paper.

It includes hundreds of topic questions, with space to jot down notes about each topic as it applies to your life. The book also explains how to compile all your stories into a cohesive book, whether you want one book or hundreds.

LifeNotes is not *only* for those who have already lived a full life – it's for everyone! Begin now to record your experiences as they happen – while the memories are fresh.

Give your family the legacy of a lifetime... *your* lifetime... in LifeNotes!

To order, see contact info below.

LifeNotes Leader's Guides

Earn extra money by starting a LifeNotes Writers Circle in your area

LifeNotes Writers Circles are groups of 6 to 15 members who meet on a regular basis. Its members share their written stories, and provide feedback to each other.

A LifeNotes leader does not need to be experienced in teaching, but merely needs to be people-oriented and able to guide the group. The leader may purchase the participant workbooks (either *LifeNotes* or *Write Your Life Story in 28 Days*) at a discount and sell at retail price, and may charge for classes and workshops as well.

For more information on becoming a LifeNtoes Writers Circle leader, please contact us (see below.)

Seminars / Workshops / Speaking

To have us put on a life-writing workshop or seminar, or to speak to your group or organization, please contact us at:

www.mylifenotes.com/deedees44@hotmail.com/480 703-1244

Printed in the United States
112642LV00005B/68/P